Praise for *Crucible Womb*

"Jill Marlene puts her soul out in front of her and follows, with authenticity and courage. Her words challenge us, the readers, to dare to go to the deepest, most dangerous parts of ourselves. She is a treasure."

—Jeanmarie Simpson, Theatre Artist

"Jill Marlene has a gift for expressing the range of the human psyche with beauty and depth. She has a mastery of the language and a gift for delivering insights into the deepest parts of who we are. Her poetry can move you emotionally and spiritually, because her words encompass the true experience of the ups and downs and interconnectedness of humanity."

—Christian Conte, PhD, Therapist, Speaker, and author of *Advanced Techniques for Counseling and Psychotherapy*

"Jill Marlene's poems are songs of human interconnection, deeply rooted in the power of the natural world. They are "we" poems, both embracing and contemplative. As fingers might trace an old scar or explore the body of a new lover, these poems address both the gamble and pain of human experience with humility and grace."

—Charles O'Hay, author of *Far From Luck*

Crucible Womb

by

Jill Marlene

A Lucky Bat Book

Crucible Womb
Copyright © 2014 by Jill Marlene

All rights reserved.

Cover Design by Dave Cherry

Cover and Interior Photos by Kaitlin Oki and Michael Mac Millan

Published by Lucky Bat Books
LuckyBatBooks.com

10 9 8 7 6 5 4 3 2 1

ISBN: 978-1-939051-86-8

This book is also available in digital format

Contents

Acknowledgements	ix
Thank You	xi
Foreword	xii
Introduction	xiv
Who?	xvi
Chapter One	**1**
November 1, 2012	2
The Minor Second Conundrum	3
Ravages	5
Changing The Story...	7
Summer Tease	8
Unsettled	9
Fox News	10
Nightmare Crucible	11
Omen	12
Chapter Two	**13**
Untitled	14
Regift	16
Syntheses	17
Mirage and Mirror	18
Snow	19
Thirsty	20
Transition	21
Untitled	22
Care	23
Lilacs Waiting	24
Garden Preacher	25
Dichotomy's Cowboys	26
The Dark Place	27
Chapter Three	**29**
Locus Limerick	30
A Haiku of Breaking the Homeostatic Cycle...	31

Spring Cleaning	32
Harvest	33
An Ode to Projective Identification	34
An answer to an Ode to Projective Identification	35
Scapegoats	36
For Joy	37
Bullies	38
The Soulscouts Code	39
Pedestals	40
Goodnight Cricket	41
Hole in the Soul… Ode to the Pedagogy of Othering	42
CHAPTER FOUR	**44**
No Reason at All	45
Appreciation	46
Mundane	47
Life Lessons from Paint	48
Back to the Grind	49
Impostors	50
Two Poems in the Style of Ogden Nash	51
Sandpaintings	52
CHAPTER FIVE	**53**
Getting There	54
We Are	55
Who Knows…	56
The Fate Testers Search	57
Heart Hearth Harvest	58
Chronic Pain	59
The Triangle	60
Pain	61
For Girls	62
Us	63
CHAPTER SIX	**64**
Another Mother's Song of Letting Go. To the inner child	65
Untitled	68

The Fledglings. Or, My midlife crisis poem.	69
The Crucible of Parenthood	70
A Visit to the Music Center After the Children have Grown	72
CHAPTER SEVEN	**75**
Forever Again	76
I Awoke to a Cup of Mulled Cider	77
Experiential	79
Advice	80
Adventure	81
April 2009	82
Break	83
Watching You Sleep...	84
Wind	85
Passion	86
Romance	87
CHAPTER EIGHT	**88**
American Girl is an Oyster	89
Man's Whirled	91
She	92
Isness	94
On	95
Spring Song	96
Tyranny	97
For Lily. My Pug and My Friend.	99
Whose life teaches me every day.	99
About the Photographers	103
Kaitlin Oki 103	
Michael Mac Millan 104	
About Jill Marlene	105

Acknowledgements

First, to my children: Robin, for the wisdom and the wonder; Gabriel, for the depth and the soulfulness; and Elaina Joy, for the insight and the presence and ALL of you for the MUSIC and the FAMILY. You have been the greatest inspiration to self-discovery that I have ever experienced. You three people crystallize the meaning of life to me. Your intelligence and uniqueness are treasures forever. NONE of this writing would have been possible without you.

To Michael Mac Millan for being my muse and the number 8.

To Kaitlin Oki for the visions.

To Kate Manning for the future.

To all the musicians, artists, and dancers who play with me and help make our collages of sound and thought.

To Tom Gordon: my lifelong friend and unconditional funk/soul brother.

To Shelly and Renee and Laura for their love of the language. It has taught me deeper respect.

To every educator I have had who has echoed and profoundly expanded my intuition that there is more to the world than polarity. Steve Hayes, Linda Hayes, Tom Harrison, Livia D'Andrea, Christian Conte, Jill Packman, and Beattyanne Rasmussen, for escorting me well into the worlds I KNEW were there but had not yet navigated with the right tools.

To James E. Carr for teaching me Functional Analysis—bringing a delightful pragmatism to the contextualism I had been flirting with for my whole life. Thank you for helping make that real for me. It finds its way into my thoughts and my writing every day.

To Shelly Marcum and Rachel Schopen for giving me the help and confidence I needed.

To the feminists and the lovers and the parents and the counselors and the contextualists, the choir directors and the actors, the behaviorists and the secular humanists, the theoretical physicists, the gardeners, the artists, and the veterinarians.

To Dave Cherry, whose artistic vision always expands my ideas to their right size and shape.

To Cindie Geddes for believing in this book and in me.

To my sister Kris, for surviving with me.

And.

To my mother, Dorthiann, for finding herself and making that process as transparent as possible.

—*Jill Marlene*
jillyflower@charter.net

Thank You

Is such an exquisite pairing of words

But, as it is

With so many words,

Our sensitivity to the richness of

History and meaning

Diminishes with use.

To rediscover and treat

the mantra of gratitude

with the proper reverence

I now intend them as if

They had never before been uttered.

Thank you.

Foreword

Not everyone is a poet, yet we all have profound insights and communion with the infinite and secret internal places, sizeless, extraordinary spaces inside our psyches we scarcely know exist; but only a small number of humans have the courage and skill to open and artfully share the contents of those confines, people we call poets; and even a rarer number of the species can turn that gaze outward on the wider universe with the same honesty and intensity and adequately express their findings in words. Jill Marlene is one of those poets.

    I met Jill when I recorded her reading several short stories for the literary magazine of sound I edit and produce, My Audio Universe. She impressed me with how well she understood the stories and their subtle meanings and moods and read them with perfectly matched cadences and emphases.

    During a subsequent recording session, Jill mentioned that she has been writing poetry for decades and is just now putting together a book-length collection. I was skeptical. As an editor who systematically reads a broad spectrum of literary magazines, a goodly percentage of contemporary poetry is wrongly categorized as poetry and is best suited for a personal journal. Nevertheless, as a favor to Jill, I agreed to read a few of her poems and was thrilled not to find what I expected.

Instead I found poems that point the lens of clarity and painful truth inward in a way that is not maudlin or self-absorbed. Jill's poems illuminate the places and things that are deeply common to the human condition, and with these ordinary elements, she creates something greater than the sum of its parts. Her words take us to the places and show us the things inside ourselves that we, as a species, are afraid to think about or even acknowledge. I was proud to publish audio of thirteen Jill Marlene poems in April 2013.

In a broader sense, Jill's poems are a beautifully colored reflection of the universe around us. From them, you know she is a single mother of three raising children in a world of crass, normalizing forces. Through the poems, she and the reader search for love and meaning as fellow commodities, and the words and ideas collectively work as an antidote for the blind violence of efficiency that scuffs and cuts without discrimination. In every poem the reader can feel the glare of the big gnarly eye that bears down on us all, yet there is redemption and hope, and with art and compassion, Jill shows us how to reconcile our plight at the limits of morality.

—*Brian Bahouth*

Introduction

Most of this poetry was written while working on my second masters degree. This one, in marriage and family therapy, came about as a culmination of a lifelong interest in art, philosophy, feminism, culture, behavior, anthropology, love, family, and most of all, my FELLOW HUMAN BEINGS. Psychotherapy is, in my opinion, applied philosophy. The training is unique in that we must learn to navigate the unknowable waters of the subjective and phenomenological world of another person. This charge carries the immense responsibility of self-awareness and self-exploration. It requires a commitment to allowing and understanding one's own place in the moment and what our place is doing to that moment. It is with the deepest respect and humility that I move into that career and that way of being.

This poetry is largely a reflection of the journey. These words were also grown in the fertile soils of Motherhood, Feminism,

Introspection, Integration of Opposites Behaviorism, Archetypes, Intersubjectivity, and most of all, the utility and futility of language.

Each poem was written from a moment where words collided with experience, and where metaphor patiently revealed the truth of that moment to me. Sometimes it is absurd and sometimes it is quite serious and at all times it is a trace of a real personal phenomenon. A real moment.

Thank you very much for reading and sharing these moments with me.

—Jill Marlene, August 2013

Who?

We are the Sistern of the Cistern

Who together knit the crucible womb

of changing hearts

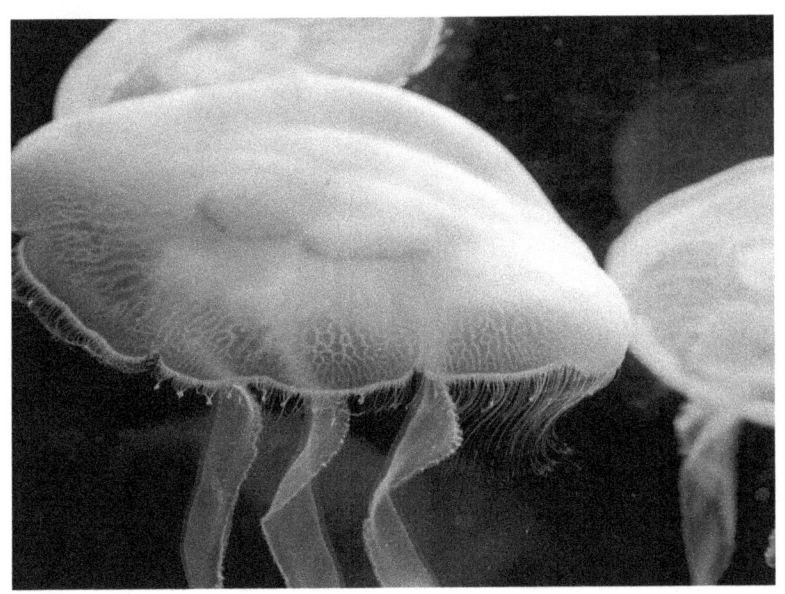

Chapter One

To keep all the fear from stealing your hours

Give it some space but don't give it power.

November 1, 2012

This cold is an angry Englishman on a lonely bus.
Bloated from private drink and arrogance,
    he stops kindred exchange with his frosty glare.
He freezes the smiles with his derision.
    The ride is long
and the shared destination is a pesky irony.
How could he be going the same direction?
how could his goals be my goals?
In a moment of unconsciousness,
as the cold enmires me,
I find myself his mirror.
    Resentful and frigid with bitterness.
When I awake to my visage
    contorted by this unseemly connection,
I force the cracking and soften from within.
    I bristle against the withering glare,
I muster a smile.
    I send forth my warmth
in the face of this sterile adversity.
    I may not soften his countenance,
But I will not let his bitterness claim me this day.
    I will accept that it must be what it is.
This cold gentleman has his purpose
    and I may gain by melting within—
before him.

The Minor Second Conundrum

The Minor Second Conundrum
pits sounds against one another
in discord. Delicious and untenable.
Vacillating
between major and minor—the chord resolves.
Exhausted from the chaotic dance
mismatched tones rubbing raw
against the listening air.
    The cello weeps—a sicksweet serenade.
    a tribute to the lover of the damned.
The harmonies condense like spotlights
illuminating
each tepid rationale.
Each practiced phrase.
Each desperate resolution.

We sing. The lies
luxuriate in night's false security
    Light of morning..
would you show your face?
Without the trumpet's fanfare Just reveal.
Such a hard fight for the
heartsong that would not live
....despite a hero's work to give it breath.
Until a melody is sung
that does not fear the dissonance
I will be the necromancer of sordid stories.
    the mirror's jest. The fools heroic calamity

The martyr's milky breast that spills untaken.
> the lone lovesong left.
> For this insipid motif sings itself.

again and again
until we each embrace our own
> unfettered melody and find harmony

in cacophony's clumsy caress.

Ravages

To the fear in the heart that has been broken,
I wish I could speak a confidence of trust.
Where trust is gone,
shields are quick and ubiquitous.
To take away that brittle shield
Is to melt away what is proud
to show what that pride disguises.

And if there is no soft place to land
already love-born in the spiny heart,
The breath gets quick
and the next available feeling
comes to take pride's place.
Anger disguises fear.
And fear disguises shame.

The shame of having been branded
with a deep sense
of worthlessness
when shame no longer describes and it indeed becomes.

It is the darkest lesson.
Only through fear, anger and pride
could the broken spirit be salvaged.

Love is a distant and cynical dream
in a world
where pain is forced deep beneath
the stone face of pride.

But at the root of the person
at the end of the cycle,
there is always love latent.
Waiting for the moment of relenting
the hopeless shame-shields of anger, fear and pride
cannot keep the breath from our lungs and so
they cannot keep the love from our hearts.

But It can make love unrecognizable to us.
Love seeks the vulnerable. It sighs with sadness at pride—
knowing that pride maligns it. Claims it.
Disavows its power.

A futile defense.
Love is complete and awaiting that soft landing
that can propel that spirit
Through pride and its tribal ritual
Through anger and its call for blood and blame
Into acceptance of the self
and the honest pain of mortal being.
Through right and wrong Growth
Us and them into We.
through fear into connection
through shame, into love

and by Love, into peace.

Changing The Story...

Heavy impending dark— shrouds every afternoon.
It comes so quick
with its decisive blow to light's levity.
Bludgeoning the facility of day
    into rickety submission.
To find the solace in this pendulous opacity—
I, Like light, shall shine anyway.
I trust my darkness.
It receives and informs my light
and betwixt them
there is made a home for colors to be set against...
The tyranny of Darkness is obsolete.
To shine
in the weathered face of winter
 is to recognize what it lacks— and then
become its fulfillment.

Summer Tease

This gentle air

belies the blistered indifference of the desert.

Like a whore's translucent robe

    it seduces—

    upturned faces smile and open at the soft sun.

We are lulled like cuckolds into this serene lie.

    Enjoy the day.

    the cold sequester of delicate snow

is ensnared in a stratagem

of time and affect.

The promise of ample tomorrows

    is whisked to the periphery

beyond the moment's wicked warm.

Unsettled

The alarmed voice of the wind

Rouses and charges capriciously.

When it rests, I am startled by its silence

When it blows, I know it carries things

I know things are changing and I am comforted.

No matter whether the change bodes well or ill.

The calm between surges of intensity is a pleasant lie that

Drops my listening ear into complacency.

Life is a great drama.

Each breath is an unfolding life or death moment

The stillness is respite from its own promises.

It will not deliver us from the torrents—

It will give us the vision to navigate them.

Fox News

Leaders made of ice— children in great bodies

frozen rigid before they had a chance

to play out forms.

Some eyes do not look back when looked into.
They see what they want to see
and you are unseen and finished
before you draw breath.

The absence of conscience
    —a sign of resolve or strength
Gives them the edge.
That Je Ne Sais Quoi
Empowers them to eclipse and reduce the
peaceful warriors
to playground fodder in the unwary eye.

And to their mockingbird melody,

we fall in line behind the minstrels

bloated in our mesmerized stupor.

We worship

These filmy heroes of the one way mirror.

Nightmare Crucible

Sweet are the dreams
that tell the stories you dare not...

Slapping open with quick brilliance
the realms undisturbed
where balrogs and hungry wolves
claw at the clever trap doors.

Washed as though by daylight,
our demons cannot hide from us in dreams.

Love the nightmare.
She comes to set you free.

Omen

Normal mortals open horror portals.

War force provoking

lordly jocund warbles,

And floral chortles—

Over prone and

open voiceless corpses.

Chapter Two

Trying to use language

to expose dialectical tension

is like trying to use a photograph

to smell a lilac

Untitled

Introspection is a skill.
It is like soul yoga.
Necessary to mind flexibility.
It is through the critical
and loving regard for self
that we maintain balance
between the within and the without.

If looking within is made impossible
by an inability
to perceive oneself in one's being
If the voice that speaks in the cells and past the story
is muted by the deafening echoes of survival states—
Brittle our hearts become
Laquered for hollow preservation.
Suspended in formaldehyde
Comfortably dying in stasis.

With Contexts contained, History embalmed
The Liquid Wonder flash frozen
We feign a separation.
No peeking
beneath the comfort shroud of feeling states—

One can fall prey
to the viscosity of fixed identity
Then, enmired in polarity and
projection,

Crucible Womb

rigidity claims the self
and others become extensions of our solipsism
rather than soulful partners in a world of mutuality.

Regift

On a binary scale
of valued opposites,
when one is relegated to a side
it is no small matter.
based on things beyond one's control,
balance may be restored
by reclaiming the devalued,
reevaluating and revaluing
inclusive of all attributes
 and all shades of permutation
between perceived antitheticals.

Syntheses

I am today the synthesis of opposites
and the restoration of a sundered self.
I am seamlessly scarred.
I am a labyrinth and a roadmap.
I can read my history in the veins of my arms,
the wrinkles on my skin,
the cracks in my voice and the wonder in my words.
I am making the choice today to be revealed.
To live out.

Mirage and Mirror

The Dazzling Display
That cloaks the fragmented soul.
Many seductive guises
Usurp and connive.
Armor that protected
Now grows into tender flesh.
Protection
Forcing Projection
Forcing Rejection.
The Rubik's Cube's Cubic Rube.
Who deftly juggles
    The Jester
    The Prince
    And the Whipping Boy
The holy trinity of sundered selves.

Snow

Hush.

Listen as the Snowflakes negotiate their descent.

Puzzle pieces

Clicking neatly next to next.

They ascend again

Piling like blankets

Bringing the earth skyward.

Thirsty

The thirsty willow shoots her unseen
deep into the ground
Her lissome fingers whip and anguish
with a whistle sound
Rooted, Fettered, Fixed and bound
with nothing to sustain
She just lets go for wintertime
will bring the rain again.

Transition

How tenderly this Fall has drawn us
to the darker days.
She's brushed the crystal frost across like
whispered loving praise.
Ephemeral deciduous
so slowly changing hue
The Winter waits
outside the gates

just taking in the view.

Untitled

The prescient wind

thrusts wildly

into my walls

foretelling changes

and mocking that

which thinks itself unchanging.

Care

    Days unfold not unlike roses.
The care I have taken in knowing
and responding to what is needed,
    the capricious fluctuations
of earth and sky
and the natural direction
    of the individual
all feature in the array that presents.

Lilacs Waiting

This surprise snow
    hushes the brazen lies of untimely spring.
    It tells its quiet truth
and slows the racing blood— quickened by false promise.
    Illusion's chilly whistleblower
    bids us "Wait!"
"Remember"
"Steady"—
And I, grateful for my lilacs' reticence,
    aquiesce into a cup of tea
and a deep sigh of relief.

Garden Preacher

Our garden
is an evangelist
drawing disciples to the soil—
patiently preaching its earthy salvation.
Its gentle language
weaves a fecund truth
from the loamy, humble pulpit.
Our grateful, quaking fingers
tickle in this common grace.

Dichotomy's Cowboys

Riders of the pendulum
swing between and through.
Only at the end
when an opposite emerges
is there a solid projection of real.
Only when we seem to stop.
We look around cautiously
and see the extreme
and unsustainable.
The disproportion of is-ness becomes daunting
Under the captivity of frozen moments.
The potential
To be fixed and immutable.
Fear and judgment comes with the illusion
that the polarity is the reality of the whole.
Then we move again
Yee Haw.

The Dark Place

There is a great peace
in knowing that it is not always the time
to be at peace...

Effortless isometric tension.
Relenting to that which must be suffered.
Relief is to know that sometimes—
it is the time be desperately sad,
Unsettled
Uncomfortable
Overworked
Underslept.
There is something beautiful
about embracing the conditions
that we are 'conditioned' to try to avoid.
It. Is.
A tangible value.
When this Present is accepted,
The Phallic Palace of Shoulds and Musts
crumbles into a bubbling rubble
and eventually disintegrates
into the flux of the functional now.

This opening is where creation begins.
The projection of a life
devised and concocted from fragments
of an unattainable Ideal
and in servitude

to avoidance of the Feeling, Breathing NOW—
Becomes a life beyond projection.
Born at each moment
and deeply lived.

Chapter Three

Steering the response

Bravely out of tested grooves

Remapping the self

Locus Limerick

When it comes to control, seems we focus,
on an outer or internal locus
whichever we follow,
the meaning is hollow
cuz it's both and there's no hocus pocus.

Crucible Womb

A Haiku of Breaking the Homeostatic Cycle...

Steering the response—
Bravely out of tested grooves.
Remapping the self.

Spring Cleaning

Sorting is a godlike act.

Determining which shreds of memory remain

In the queue of continued contact

And which are banished netherward to oblivion

Value of life or death granted

By a casual gesture

toward the shelf or the trashcan.

Harvest

The Harvest of introspection is our talisman.
A reminder of the summer fruit
and then the heavy dark
that teaches with thick breath
and deep sunken feet.
The twilight sleep that hides the world
only so that our finding
should grow stronger.
It reveals as we adjust.
It obscures when we succumb
to the tyranny
of form over function.

An Ode to Projective Identification

I've always loved the broken boys.
The ones whose parents broke their joy
Or those who couldn't seem to find,
In direst need, a gentle mind.

Who carved their personhood from thoughts
And forced their feelings into aught,
And I've believed with all my heart,
With open hand and graceful art,

These boys would see within my eyes—
That who they are is recognized.
But now I know that they must see
What brings familiarity.

So by the rigid lens and vice—
the truth of me is twisted twice.
Once to show his feelings' face
and then to take his feelings' place.

No matter how it splits from truth,
The damage done in wretched youth
Defies the strongest love embrace
And through the damage, love's erased.

An answer to an Ode to Projective Identification

So Where am I in all of this
What is my part ? what did I miss?
I think my fear of causing harm
allows me to fall to this charm

I want to love I want to heal
but stay with love when it's not real.
My father's touch my limits crossed
Is most relived when I am lost.

And the more I try to stand
And keep myself to my command
I let the judgment and the scorn
decide for me and I am torn.

And so I let projections be
And let his judgment stagger me.
Then I surrendered, seek embrace?
And love within an empty face.

Within myself the doubts and fears
the wretched voices drawing tears
Say I deserve to be alone.
if I make my desire known.

Scapegoats

All Hail the Scapegoats—

the ones who see
The Elephant In The Room.

The ones who cry for help
While the shackle of shame
is tied around the family's hearts.

The ones that are on the receiving end
of the pointed finger.

They are the key to possibility.

To freedom
from the tyranny of silence
and false fronts.

They are the symptom—

the secret to of the sickness

that betrays the system.

For Joy

I seek the resilience to remain ever present to my life.

I seek the humility to live life on life's terms

I seek the flexibility to evolve along with life.

In spite and because of its challenges.

I seek the love to embrace life always in all ways.

Bullies

Proactively Standing for yourself does not make you a bully. No matter how much real bullies say so.

Asking for congruence or to have incongruence explained
Is not 'controlling' another.
No Matter how many hypocrites say so

And honestly expressing yourself is not being arrogant
No matter how many insecure people say so.

The Soulscouts Code

Through all adversity,
I promise—to remain vulnerable,
> to differentiate from the tacit programming
> of my culture of origin—
to question myself to allow the self that can be.
> To create peace
> without fear
or avoidance of conflict
but to use conflict to grow...
To stand for myself with strength and without rigidity.
To find the well of love in pain
and open to its power.
And to see the perfection in every moment.

Pedestals

I am very pleased
    to have fallen off of so many pedestals...
    the earth underfoot is authentic.
The attention of those
who project the ideal onto another
is fleeting and shallow.
Though it feels, for a moment, like deep acceptance
it could not be a greater deception.
It is a call to conform.
    To be that which is desired.
That which lies outside one's own process.
The less attachment
    I have to the appraisal of me by others,
the closer and kinder I am to myself.
If I lose your interest the more you know me,
the luckier I am indeed.

    I will not take for granted your appraisal
    of how it affects you,
I do not wish to cause harm.
I will just allow you to decide
    whether I am what you believe me to be
and whether any judgments of incongruity
are your responsibility
or mine.

Goodnight Cricket

A Soloist
resolute
and rigid in his cadence.
Bellows a bolero
of desperate desire
that asserts itself, brazen,
before the waning.
His orchestra
bounces doubletime beneath him
Conducted
with urgency
to help him elude
the lonely sleep to come.

This shrill diva wears out the refrain.

To love one last time.
To make the legacy.
To hide the spectre
of frosty impotence.

And the big bawdy love song
beds down deep in the radical stillness
of the late summer desert.

a lot of noise.
For such a little thing.

Hole in the Soul... Ode to the Pedagogy of Othering

For those of us who've been removed
from feelings into 'what behooves'
And other's gazes held above
Our need for comfort, warmth or love.

It is a bit more difficult
to tell from what the ache results
Is it a want? is it a need?
Whence comes the hungers we must feed?

We may not know when it's too much
We may not question testing touch.
We may not know our own desire
We can't distinguish ice from fire.

And we may gorge ourselves or drink,
and not know when we're at the brink
We may not know when we've enough
We cannot call the liar's bluff.

We echo in our crystal minds
The crippling words they left behind.
"You don't need that!" "Those tears aren't real"
"I've had enough of how you feel!"

When we asked, "Mommy, what is wrong?"
Her face enraged, her temper strong,
And she said "Nothing!!!!! Go away!"
And then, with shame our hearts would pay.

Crucible Womb

Confused, Conflicted, Angry, Sad,
So much too much for mom and dad,
They stay inside and there they burn
And this is how our spirits learn.

That we must now anticipate
The needs and wants of friend or mate
and if we ever get it wrong,
we won't be loved, we won't belong.

But we can never get it right,
So day by day and night by night
We watch ourselves fragmented, try
To find our being through others' eyes.

When in the mirror, in our thoughts
In our bodies all in knots,
The precious clues to self persist
proclaiming softly, "I EXIST!"

Chapter Four

No one tells

the vanilla bean to be cocoa.

    but she shows up

fearlessly in the chocolate cake.

No Reason at All

I've one beloved pair of socks
They've walked all over grass and rocks
and yes, o'er carpet, snow and dirt
They now have holes... oh how it hurts.

I have another BORING pair
No hearts and pink—no special flare.
I have a wicked evil plot
To save my stockings that are shot...

The unworn socks, I'll slice the soles
And make my frankenstockings whole.
And when I wear them all will plead
"Where did you get those socks, we need!!!"

And at my shoes, I'll gaily grin
and think about the gore within.
I'll look them up and down and say,
"you wouldn't want them anyway."

Appreciation

We are so far detached from death,
We take for granted sacred breath
But if to breathing we attend
We worry so that it will end
Why can't we celebrate it all
And just enjoy the rise and fall
And when at last is still the breast
We have with stillness then been blessed.

Mundane

Sometimes,
when I look out my bedroom window,
the hue of the morning sky
excites me like the
first glimpse of the roller coasters
when approaching amusement parks.
The air suddenly offers greater nourishment
    and there is an urgency in my eyes
    as if they are pulling me
with total abandon by the heart.

This is a beautiful day.

Life Lessons from Paint

For optimal bonding,
Prepare the original surface well
make sure there is no residue
that, though perhaps invisible,
    might interfere with attachment.

Back to the Grind

The paintsanding kind
The stripping of old paint and dirt left behind
So brightly that reflected sun makes you blind
So I do not mind that I'm falling behind,
I will get it all done for
I am so inclined.

Impostors

There was a shrewd fictitious rose,

Of little note to eye or nose,

That through my rosebush wove about

And tried to squeeze MY roses out!

It mocked their habits— stole their earth

and flowered full with greedy girth

And so, for years I did not see

I gardened round it— let it be.

Today its swindling stalks I found

And ripped it bloody from the ground.

Two Poems in the Style of Ogden Nash

.It's on this day, I skip and dash,
  they've said I write like Ogden Nash!
And you may ask, "well, who is he?
and I will say... "He writes like me."

Noble creatures are the pugs,
    they snore like pigs, they lie like rugs.
Their bulging eyes, their wrinkled skin,
their tendency to be... not thin.
Some find it nice, some find it sick
when one another's eyes they lick.
And when I speak, their heads they cock,
    As if they listen when I talk.

Sandpaintings

Ephemeral beauty

whose influence persists

in the consciousness

of the corporeal continuum

The Illusive and elusive

Beingness.

The challenge to permanence

that indicates it.

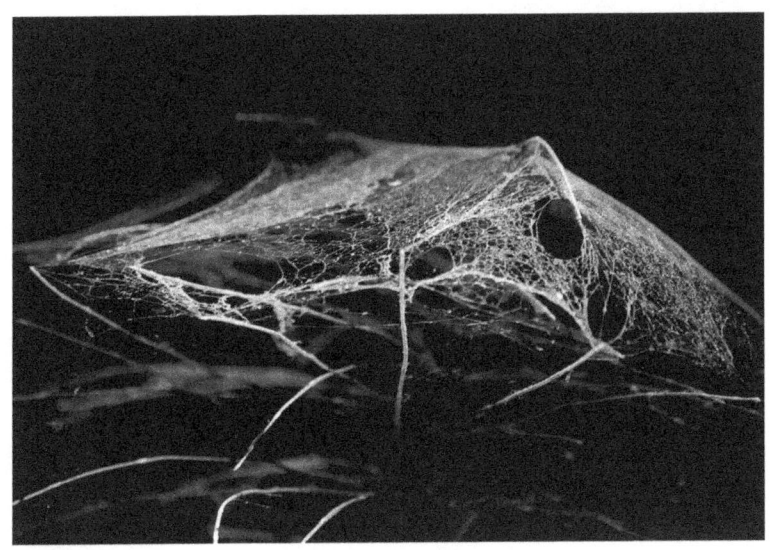

Chapter Five

To exist requires breathing.

    To live requires breathing consciously.

Getting There

Some people cannot or will not Become...
    It is our task to be as true to ourselves
and our values as we can be.
    To have integrity with regard to our feelings and actions.

    And should others choose
to continually deny our subjective experience
To shut the door on self awareness through introspection and courage,
then we must release them

to their own self inflicted pain.
No matter how it hurts us.
And though we love them,
The circle of their periphery—

Their concentric relationship to us
may be distanced.
Boundaries are,
so that we may be.

We Are

Extending
> the reach of our embrace.

Transcending
> the speech that made us brace,

Attending
> to teach and learn the pace,

Defending
> the dream we dare to chase,

and Mending
> the breach to take our place.

Who Knows...

I go in phases like the moon,
There are those times when I'm in tune
With all the subtle whispered grace,
The gravity of time and space
The depth of Shadow's dark device
And meanings turned and rendered thrice—
And then again the circle's dance
Brings me to wordless happenstance
I trip and tarry, spin and weave
Mundane, I to my comforts cleave
And I in discomposure, strive
And to my wonder, still arrive.
For wisdom does not only speak
To people who, surrendered, seek.
It will commune through any voice
by reckless chance or conscious choice.

The Fate Testers Search

for Gaps in solid ground.
With Zephyr's
intensity they falter or stand

The Real manifests.
Sigh relief through the bruises.
The secret keeps itself.
The real we find is the real we knew
before we could speak.
And for those to who, life has been most cruel,
Fate is cast until Testing breaks—
Or helps us find another real.

Heart Hearth Harvest

Cloud goddesses of spun silver,
their breath the air
over mountain creeks
    their eyes of galaxies.
Looking kindly down,
tickling you playfully with their treasure mist.
caressing your face
with dewy generous hands.
Songs of fortune and adventure
fill your ears, serenity fills your heart.
And you are
soul—lifted to see the worlds
that you have touched...
brightened and broadened.
Crystal fountains twinkling
secret messages of gratitude and promise.
A velvet cornucopia forms bursting at your feet. Your
Harvest is at hand.

Chronic Pain

I wait and I wait
for the pain to abate
It is stronger of late.
thinking on this strange fate
why is this on my plate?
why this hurt I must sate?
How to ameliorate?
With no system to rate?
nor an obvious gate?
I must re-integrate
give it love and not hate
and not anticipate—
Give it space to create.

The Triangle

They Say You and me
and the devil make three"
    BUT when I stop blaming
the devil or thee,
then I can be me—
and you can be thee.
The devil may be—
only if we agree—
that I cannot be
much of me without thee.
And when I am free
to accept me as me
and to love thee as thee—
of the devil we're free!

Pain

Pain.

My consort, my enemy.

my ally against complacency.

My distant sister of maleficence

wielding her cruel and necessary ridicule

like an indolent bully.

For Girls

The dewy maiden never really played in light of day.
a mother's milky need emerged and wrested her away.
And so it is with all the girls whose mothers, wracked with fear
were never there to lead the way or make the meadow clear.

Some of these mother / children knew advantage may be lost
the power of their beauty— might be worth their children's cost?
The glamour may provide the cover needed to deceive
But everyone who looks within will no longer believe.

And so these mother / babes persist in rosy lip and cheek
And draw to them the kinds of friends who only beauty seek.
A parlour full of mirrors and a pocket full of time,
The artisans of archetype the damsels of design.

I will not grasp this momentary ease of worldly gains
but open up the world to those for whom the world remains.
Whatever loveliness of face remains when I am grown
I hope is incidental to my wise and weathered crone.

Us

Lucky is he
and lucky is she—
who seek no single key,
    to be higher than thee—
but to really just be...
And to seek to be free,
The completeness of "me"
in the context of we.

Chapter Six

Breach Barriers

By Being Boldly

Beneficent.

Become Brethren.

Birth Belonging.

　　　　Byproduct? Bliss. Blessed be.

Another Mother's Song of Letting Go. To the inner child

A syndicate of vigorous youth
Casual and confident,
Graces my living room tonight.
They are brimming with lust for freedom
They can smell it
so close.
So close are their noses
to what they yearn to taste.
Anise and lemon balm
are earthy impostors
of silky, candied promises.

Gritty and fibrous,
they demand the effort of discernment.
Their treats are hard won
The tongue does not quite enjoy the fulfillment
of the heart's expected, easy, (if hollow,) sweet.

The phantom licorice and lemon tart
lasciviously beckon through the olfactory looking glass
The imagined world of endless abandon
The candyland of unfettered
Sweet that Never Sours
Pleasure that never lies.
This Witch's Turkish Delight
is a cheap seduction.

Peel away the wrapper.
Experience and Expectation will wrestle
Vying for dominance
like rivals in a legacy.
Let them fight it out
while we watch.
Experience will win and we go home richer.

Open Your Oyster with wonder.
Know that what is taken is changed.
And as you take what you will,
know that you alter the world.
Honor the taking. So to comfort the child
who stands in total amazement
at your strength and sense of place.
The child that you threaten to leave in your blustery wake...
He is there to keep you kind.

Take this self with you,
for he is in you—
Reminding you forever
To give deep attention to moments—in the vastness of ages.
Hold him loving and close
as you navigate, together, the realms
between the invincible juggernaut of burgeoning self—
and the fragile fallibility of the infant soul.
Let him hold your gaze
low and sweetly awake—
that you may always know the joy
of seeing for the first time.

Crucible Womb

Hold him high—
that he may know the larger view.
And together,
hold the soft, supple gaze
of discovery without conquest
Tractile and steadfast
in the service of all aspects of harmony.
And the two of you shall celebrate
the imperfect evolution
of a mind that loves
a heart that thinks
and a self that deeply lives.

Untitled

Last night I dreamed of giving birth...
The solid weight and pelvic girth
the frightened joy, the grateful bliss
the waiting for the face to kiss.

I felt him heavy, like a stone
I felt the creaking of the bone
I felt the pressure and the heat
—so blinding, urgent ...no retreat.

There is no rest from swollen ache
and knowing that your flesh will break
and yet there is this gorgeous, clear
and primal voice that Mothers hear.

My answers... moans of deadly deep
would wind me in and out of sleep
and with my hand I felt his head
Between my legs on forest's bed.

And held within the Mother's fold
There played the tale so often told
The one that no descriptions serve
This singularity of nerve.

With steel's resolve and water's force
This person did my womb divorce
And gave me something precious dear
his perfect, lucid, living tears.

The Fledglings. Or, My midlife crisis poem.

The looming empty nest is shaken all around
by a sentient wind that predicts deep
and unavoidable transformation.
Our Microcosm expands without us.
The hole that is left
will be ever refilling and emptying again
accommodating an evolving love.
New scenes will be played
with different players
in the hallowed spaces
with the poster plastered walls.
New objects and new conversations.
But These rooms will always be open.
These rooms are ever in the mothers flesh
And will become relics— places to revisit.
to reminisce and explore the impossibility of past selves.
Sacred spaces filled with treasures of heart's antiquity.
And the fledglings who filled that space with life
now occupy a larger, deeper space.
One that contains all of that which played out
on that small, deep stage of self.
Their space is foreign to me now. not unfamiliar
these fledglings are masters of time and space.
They bilocate— living at once and at last
in worlds of their own making
and forever in the mother's soul
Becoming greater and deeper of dimension in both worlds
with each day, each choice, each breath
as a separate sovereign self.

The Crucible of Parenthood

It is such an honor
To stand watch over a life.
To be the place
from which a person can go
to explore their becoming
and to which they return
at the end of each adventure.

To embody the delicate and delicious dance
of letting go and holding on.
To know that the ultimate goal
is make oneself unnecessary.
And to strive for obsolescence as if it was immortality itself.

To be carried beneath the conscious
in each introspection and each expression
but to never be a burden to the autonomous self.

To be invisible but ever present,

To infuse
but never usurp.

To be There
in what ever way is needed
and not have this needing become us.

To be completely connected to the self
and completely committed to Love's unfolding

Crucible Womb

as to weather gracefully
the ten-thousand severances of Becoming.

This is a charge worthy of reverence.

A Visit to the Music Center After the Children have Grown

Maytan's music center floods me with history.
Endless hours waiting outside classroom doors
    for the juicy moments of musical growth.
The smell of wood and paper
in this building that has seen decades of weather and life.

Intermittent streams of familiar music,
"april in paris" on a saxophone—
"Ode to joy" on a half sized violin—
pass through the space
    their melodic streams crossing one another
in a cacophany of individual striving.
Weaving into collective sighs of accomplishment.

The upturned faces of the children
Ask all manner of questions.
Ragged boys—Manhood eluding them
for a few more years
look to their instructors
with a tacit and ironic respect.
But not without a little resentment.

Little Girls
whose hands barely grasp the bows
screech the strings like so many angry feral cats.
Peals of laughter are the orchestral bed
underlying the playful intemperate song.

Crucible Womb

And Virtuosos—
taking a surgeon's care
choose the mouthpiece
or the stick
or the brush
or the new instrument.
I watch them purchase
what is to them a necessity.
Like a staple at the grocers.
Flour, milk, apples, reeds, strings.

For many who have not earned the prize of
mastery
or confidence through engagement—
Who have denied themselves the journey,
this kind of purchase
is a forlorn and pretentious acquisition.
Full of "later" and "Maybe"
and all the cruelty of "Someday"

But my favorite people at the music center
are those who dream with eagerness.
They exude the humility to stand before music
ready to play
and fail
and be shaped...
A better prize awaits.
Their commitment is not measured

by purchase or collection
but by a lovers' obsession.

A devotion to an immortal
yet tangible goddess.
their songs are a constant praise at the liquid alter of MUSIC.

These Lovers—
they run their fingers across the
Rubinesque curves of the acoustic guitar—
Their voices bleed with passion—
Their fingers ache for congress with the keys—
Their Hearts align with the timber and pulse—

They honor the discipline
Like a sacred vow
with their blisters
Their desire
And their time.

They are not masters over.
They are lovers with.
Lovers.
At Play.

Chapter Seven

Lilacs budding here—

there will soon be sweet breezes.

Jasmine by your door—

Olfactory stars—

Redolent of soul caress—

and the possible.

Forever Again

The diamond bleeds when breaks the Eight,

the skin recoils, the hands deflate.

The teasing tides of future fate

they crest, unwanted, and abate.

The oyster's pearl is found too late,

the lover dares not bear the weight—

But still and empty, poised and great...

the graceful hearts regenerate.

Crucible Womb

I Awoke to a Cup of Mulled Cider

It was sweet with cinnamon
clove and ginger and thoughtfulness.
Redolent of fleeting time.
Like the fickle seasons,
it teased me.
Warm in my throat
out of phase with the frigid morning.

This dissonance wakens
an ancient, dormant sadness.
The one that comes with knowing that there was something...
something left undone,
unseen?

Unfelt?

Like a sleepy lullaby in another tongue
that offers no tether to the familiar waking world—
but seduces into opacity nonetheless.
I missed the marker.
I must have slept through the passage.
I did not hear the alarm.

Clumsy,
I slipped on my memory
past the turnstyle

into the next morning.
I entered having not paid the toll.
Nor read the map.
With my sweet cup of time,
Unprepared, and anxious
into the snow.

Experiential

And still there is the truth of our innocence
The truth of our chance to be revealed
To ourselves
Through our love,
Our Anger
Our Longing
Our Passion.
For this I would wear the white dress every day.
But the love is here
In Me.
The mirrors are ubiquitous
And the lover brings another fertile chance to love
From every place within.

Advice

Some people lie without even knowing it.
Some are truthful for simplicity's sake.
And others tell the truth out of compulsion.
Still others doubt themselves out of
respect for their own fallibility.
Still others lie intentionally
Try to keep it contained
and then place the blame for the
lie on the one whom it affects the most deeply.
Never marry one of those.

Adventure

From the forest

where trees buckle beneath frigid blankets

To the shore

Where we watched unicorns free themselves from the

turgid froth of their sea prison.

And back again by icy black ribbon

To the brittle

crystal desert.

April 2009

This morning the suburban windchimes echo peruvian pipes.
endless unresolving joyful and morose.
b- flat— minor arpeggio in a freezing breeze.

There is a march on in this morning wind. It is headed no particular place and would wage no war or foster no sense of patriotism. It would blow for blowing's sake.

Its rhythm is particular and gravity keeps it.

I can hear you in this lonely melody.
Leaving momentstones alone ending on a question.

Unresolved and lovely. Potentiated by stirring sky.

I can smell you in the frosty wind.
Feel you in the scratch of the branch as the peach blossoms struggle to endure the relentless pummelling of the song-laden ice.

Gratitude is the color of these blossoms.
Thankful for one more night's opportunity to become.

They Must believe the songs will warm in time.

Break

Idiotic,
    startled gasps
at faulty fleeting impulse
render the foolish lover
brusquely from her waking dream.
Mourning love
is much like mourning death.
Sharp,
ubiquitous
and unrelenting.

Watching You Sleep...

While you sleep.

    I weave shimmering thoughts.

The media of which the dream is made.

And when I dream tonight,

painted silk strands

of wonder and knowing

    thrust and wind into soft air

and through the caterwaul

of ambulance siren

and desperate tires

into your vulnerable ears.

Softening the blow of the outside world

    and settling into

whispers.

Wind

Sleepy clouds
blow gentle indecision
down on the wind-weary trees.
The air is still,
    warm,
    tentative.
A wistful curtain of green
is sprayed crimson
with the rugged Hawthorne.
Thick tongues of florid branch
mock the wind and the street and above,
exhausted giants breathe
verdant sighs of surrendered grace.

Passion

Such a pretty crystal breaks the light.
Bold and brazen he lays himself coolly
upon my thirsty eye.
Timber and tone gracing the waiting air.
Songs in my ear
strings of unforgiving beauty
weave and bind my heart
to this defiant minstrel.
He smells of sandalwood and amber
and cherries and sage.
His hands are conduits of soul.
Under these hands,
skin becomes immortal.
In his kisses I taste the changing wind.
And for a precious moment, It blows just for me.

Romance

Aspen shadow quakes
make late afternoon windows
into living stained glass
of monochromatic grandeur.

This playful light tickles my bed
and quiet belies the bluster outside.

The shady forms change like summer clouds
and make stories on my sheets
in romantic black and white.

As if I may next see Errol Flynn
step though the window
from the aspen's loose camouflage
and into my dreaming room
to caress my feet and tell me all the secrets
the wind and the trees whisper
but the walls, those tales, obscure.

Chapter Eight

The maiden within,

Mother's kisses cover sweet

Birthing now the crone.

American Girl is an Oyster

Seduced by the fancy dance of the walrus' words.
booming voice of the patriarch
The stories of a titillating world where she is not safe without him
As he dons his neckerchief and pulls a knife from his pack
but he will keep her. Safe.
She is his slave dancer.
He deftly takes from her her instruments Assuring her they are unfinished.
They must be cleaned, improved.
and he plays upon his own pipe
His own thumping drum
He bids her dance and gives her leave to move
From out her storied shell trance she cracks and vulnerably
Slithers from her safety. She grows full and untethered
the rhythms fatten her need to satiate.
She does not know that his stories are crafted just so.
Just so.
Just so she forgets her own instrument—
And she moves juicy to his song rape.
And American girl excuses the plunder blunders of
American boy. She dresses in her sheath of
Blood, Jasmine and sky
stiffens the resolve with her warm echo of his brazen tattoo
and her offering of self sweetens the stench of the gotten gain
she smiles and opens her folds
he reaches in and tries to take the pearl.
Just then her song is jostled loose

and she remembers.
Her voice comes back to her and starts to weave itself around her greedy fingers.
No instrument outside,
no fecund breath runs through a hollow reed
No man required to make melody.
His gesture quakes within the loamy fold
the polished pain slips round his tepid hand
The pillage is a failure, the ecstasy in twining of the songs.
He keeps his rhythm. She exposes it
Dumb, repetitive and hypnotic—and she keeps dancing
now a melody from out her amber throat—
is strange like death
the roses you were not supposed to pick.
His Mother's Mother's garden. Plunder or to tend?
does he render the pearl free from the folds by force of his philosophy?
Or will the contralto be faintly heard
lowly moaning open.
beneath the soprano's fairy descant
and the pearl waits.
The product of the pain of deep surrender…
beauty from the force of burden's girth.
Growing and polishing itself with each undulation
the cacophony culminates in a moment of vivid understanding.
She offers the pearl, A renewable prize—forged in her own surrender
A souvenir of hard ideas pressed on tender flesh.
and American boy shies back from the harvest.
He knows that it does not belong to him.

Man's Whirled

What may we do about the need to elevate feminine values of
connection and love and nurturance.
> They hold the key to our evolution as a culture.

We, (for all the "right" reasons)
allow this love to be co-opted
with the unintended result
of maintaining a "Man's World."
One where Independence is valued over interdependence,
and the feelings and skills and strengths of one are valued over another—
> we do the world a great disservice.

We do this on a micro level in our relationships
when we allow our selves to be overrun
by our need for the "love" of someone
who does not appreciate our true value.
The wholeness of US.
We can stop this cycle forever
as mothers of our children of
as metaphorical mothers of ourselves
when we choose to look for the good and nurture it.
> We may relegate black and white thinking

and hierarchical social structure to where it belongs
Just two options among the many many possibilities of being.

She

She is the extended arm that moves the world.
And when she is defined by Man's sundered philosophy,
she becomes oppression's consort—
her gentle hands do pain's dirty work.
She scrubs away...
When rendered powerless by love's propaganda,
She becomes the scapegoat
of a thousand of His mirrored sycophants.
She is blinded and tethered to the task
of perpetually defacing herself.

> For his love, she is the force of labor
>   that drives the machine
> that undermines her progeny.
> She may undo this word woven web
> When is spoke the word, "Mother"
> she may answer with the voice of the banshee—
> And though once blinded
> for his pleasure—
> by her own hand,
> she will see beyond the rigid cathexis
> into the melting of worlds
> and she will dance in the continuum
> betwixt the brutal dichotomies.
> In the bubbling myriad of possibilities—
> her children will breathe in their own measure.
> The work will turn to affirmation of potentials.

Crucible Womb

The divisive seducer will be drained—
exhausted with no one to pick up after him.

Isness

Situation, time, place, manner?

Is there no whatwherewhen question word that fosters understanding of Kairotic being.

Oscillations and pulses of liquid soul?

Nothing is free of context

But out linguistic tools cannot describe this contexts vastness and diversity.

We could try

"IF"

But it implies "then." Which "then" becomes "what" and "when"

Is there a word that suggests exquisite anticipation of the present moment? The particle and the wave?

Maybe it just

"IS."

Crucible Womb

On

Familiar are the recycled scenes.

Weathered and wrecked is the trompe l'oeil
Which bade me avert my warier eye.

Here now is a forest of tangible magic.

The praxis of the sacred dreaming bed.

Justice done to this
Is a child that cries for the fallen butterfly—

Her Trembling outstretched heart and the
Exquisite weightless kaleidoscope.
Are not accustomed to this gravity.

And compassion calls to action.

With the talisman of memory—
"arise avowed"
No more trembling in cynical judges' gazes.

No more wallowing in this sty of Identity.

Mine, now, is to honor, to wonder, to challenge, to question,
To falter and gasp.
To love and to love that I love.

And I shall give my breath and voice to this rainbow

It will find its way back to the sky.

Spring Song

She draws a bow of Hawthorne and spider's web
across stretched ligaments
bound to a hollow conch.

Brandishing this visceral cacophony...
this aural talisman
she plays to pierce the cautious silence
that selfishly hoards fertile tears.

Winter melts,
    tears fall,
        land greens.
    And the lady opens up her throat.
Her voice is the consort of grief.
Her heartsong is a feather bed.
Come, and cry with her and rest.

Tyranny

Those who have not lived
>under the oppression of shoulds
>that is the tyranny of Man's feminine beauty
>cannot possibly know
>the subtle mummification

that happens when the idolatry of beauty splits us
from within
through dividing us without.
After all, as man has decided through his worship of polarity,
>He is intellect, She is Intuition

He is reason, She is Emotion,
He is mind, She is body.
>He is culture and She is Nature,

Our power is insulted and reduced to beauty
And beauty is reduced to the narrow scope of
what can be mastered. Controlled
Dominated.

And we condemned
live and perpetuate the story
under this divisive rubric.
If we wish to transcend this,
>Let us take the bold step
>decide to stop
>playing by those rules.

we are Nature AND culture,
Subject AND Object,
Mind AND Body.

And we begin to chip away at EITHER/OR
as the dominant way of thinking.
in a synergistic, technological world,
it won't be one or the other
of sides that wins,
it will be the one who can win, lose and sustain—
    becoming something greater.
       Inclusive of the antithesis.

Crucible Womb

For Lily. My Pug and My Friend.
Whose life teaches me every day.

Just before the day's end
when we walk
we make Long shadows.
A surreal stillness
saturates the suburban asphalt.
Her collar proudly
displays her rabies shots
her fading name
on the chipped
and tiny metal heart.
And a number— the hopeful
laser-cuts still announcing
"I belong somewhere."
Responsible owner.
This tiny dog is ancient
in her own right.

Her life—eclipsed.
Under the tyranny
of her blustery littermate
She played the sycophant.
They licked each other's
ears and eyes
They slurped
and snorted and scarfed.
He was always one step ahead.

Save for the gargantuan
yet inconsequential puppy—
Who exploded into the house
barely larger than
she when he came
And now,
who is a dragon
descending and darting
Demanding and devastating...

She is Alone.

She is now the merry widow.

Todd had been her loyal,
if often arrogant,
friend, litter mate,
constant companion—
and her oppressor.

While the blustery puppy is a hazard,
he does not tear at her awareness
he is something to which she must react
like the weather, an oncoming car.
Or one of the humans
during their messy, impulsive pubescence.

Todd had the my space page.
Todd was the KING.

Crucible Womb

Todd was the best friend
and the one
for whom the songs were written.
And when he passed into his sweet night,
all his favorite hands and hearts
were upon him.
He was the one who must be answered.
And as the needle mercifully
took his last breath

Lily slept.
Unsuspecting in the next room.

For a day,
She looked around sniffing and snorting
as if something was missing

(Even now, she licks the pillows
like she once licked the protruding eyes
of her corpulent brother.)

And yet, in days—
as the habits began to unwind themselves
in the spacious absence of the top dog,
her step began to spring.
Her face became upturned.
More eyes were looking into hers
from that direction now.

She asserts herself into the kitchen
Postures herself at the door

Lily makes her own pace now.

No need for a leash,
her following is as natural as her breath.
Grateful to her for her sweet life,
I pause in this tentative evening light.

She takes her time.
She sweetly sniffs
for the familiar and the foreign.

Her olfactory journey,
so much more sophisticated than any I could take
is not subject to the demands of her Alpha.

She struts—
as much the grande dame
as the tiny troll that folks see
as they roll by in their cars.

Tonight, as we walk, her shadow is long.
She is taller than she was.
It is golden and sweet in this light.
The sunset will be glorious.
She will twitch in her sleep...
as if tickled by memory.
I know as she slows,
as the light passes behind the last of the trees,

Her night is coming too.

About the Photographers

Kaitlin Oki

Kaitlin Oki, of Reno, Nevada, is an artist, musician and student. She is currently studying environmental science and policy and practicing photography at the University of Nevada where she acts as photo editor at the university's newspaper.

Kaitlin's Photos:

Thank You
Foreword
Chapter 1 • Chapter 2 • Chapter 3 • Chapter 4 • Chapter 5 • Chapter 6 • Chapter 7 • Chapter 8
Baseball for Lily

About the Photographers

Michael Mac Millan

Michael Mac Millan is an entrepreneur and creative spirit who was born in Sacramento, California, and has spent most of his life living between his beloved San Francisco, California, and Reno, Nevada. A student of sound engineering and the wonders of all things electrical, he is currently following a path in live sound and event coordination .

Michael's Photos

Cover
Who

About Jill Marlene

Jill Marlene is a 44-year-old mother of three, a grandmother of one, and a native Nevadan. She is currently working as a marriage and family therapy intern. She holds a second masters in behavior analysis and will be working with individuals, families, and couples. She will include as part of her practice working with those couples and families with at least one member on the Autism spectrum. She wants to use her practice as a way to help individuals enhance their ability to actively, intelligently, mindfully, and lovingly create their lives and nurture the lives of others.

Jill's inquiry into the nature of how we become who we are takes many forms. In addition to writing and psychotherapy, she also explores the world as a singer of opera, folk, Celtic, rock, and bluegrass music and sings with several ensembles. As a recording artist, she has written and recorded many songs with collaborators and friends, performed on many diverse projects such as the critically acclaimed world music project the "Psalms of Ra," which was recorded and produced at Skywalker Ranch in Marin County, California. Jill is a producer/director of music and musical theater, a belly dancer, a Yoga and Acro Yoga practitioner, a decent citizen, a gardener, and a lover of pets and very long walks. She makes her home in Reno, Nevada, with her beautiful family.

Jill also provided photos for the cover and after the Introduction

www.ingramcontent.com/pod-product-compliance
Lightning Source LLC
Chambersburg PA
CBHW031450040426
42444CB00007B/1045